FINGERPICKING
Children's Songs

ISBN 0-634-09890-X

Visit Hal Leonard Online at www.halleonard.com

HAL•LEONARD®
CORPORATION
7777 W. BLUEMOUND RD. P.O. BOX 13819 MILWAUKEE, WI 53213

INTRODUCTION TO FINGERSTYLE GUITAR

Fingerstyle (a.k.a. fingerpicking) is a guitar technique that means you literally pick the strings with your right-hand fingers and thumb. This contrasts with the conventional technique of strumming and playing single notes with a pick (a.k.a. flatpicking). For fingerpicking, you can use any type of guitar: acoustic steel-string, nylon-string classical, or electric.

THE RIGHT HAND

The most common right-hand position is shown here.

Use a high wrist; arch your palm as if you were holding a ping-pong ball. Keep the thumb outside and away from the fingers, and let the fingers do the work rather than lifting your whole hand.

The thumb generally plucks the bottom strings with downstrokes on the left side of the thumb and thumbnail. The other fingers pluck the higher strings using upstokes with the fleshy tip of the fingers and fingernails. The thumb and fingers should pluck one string per stroke and not brush over several strings.

Another picking option you may choose to use is called hybrid picking (a.k.a. plectrum-style fingerpicking). Here, the pick is usually held between the thumb and first finger, and the three remaining fingers are assigned to pluck the higher strings.

THE LEFT HAND

The left-hand fingers are numbered 1 though 4.

Be sure to keep your fingers arched, with each joint bent; if they flatten out across the strings, they will deaden the sound when you fingerpick. As a general rule, let the strings ring as long as possible when playing fingerstyle.

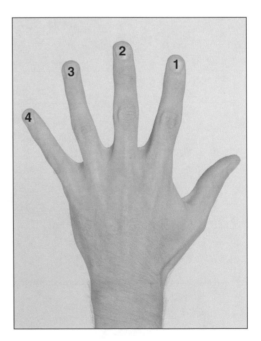

Any Dream Will Do

from JOSEPH AND THE AMAZING TECHNICOLOR DREAMCOAT

Music by Andrew Lloyd Webber
Lyrics by Tim Rice

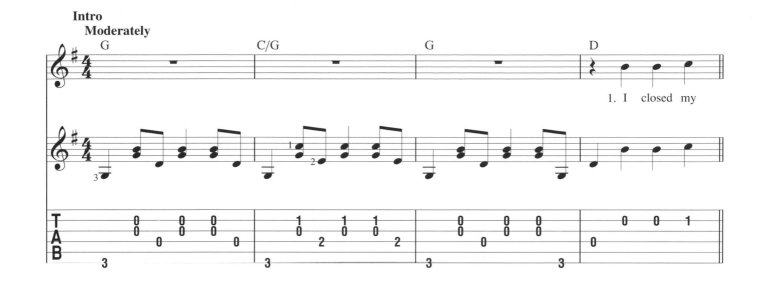

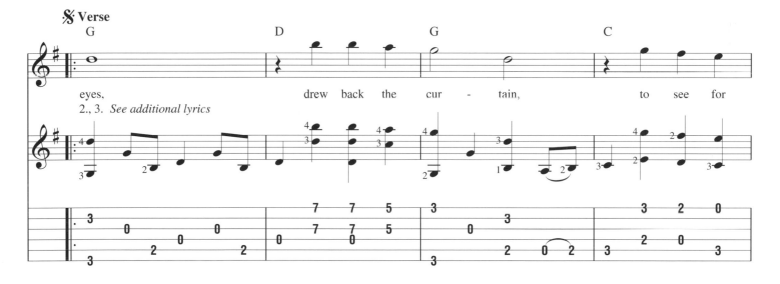

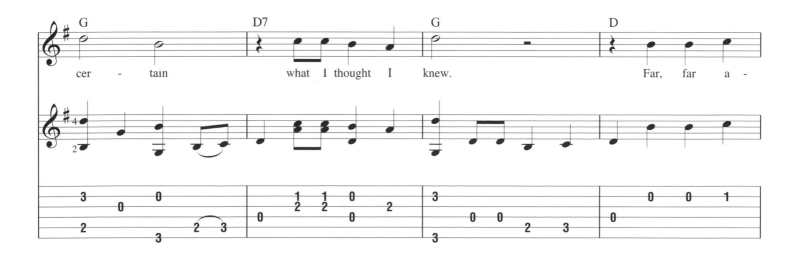

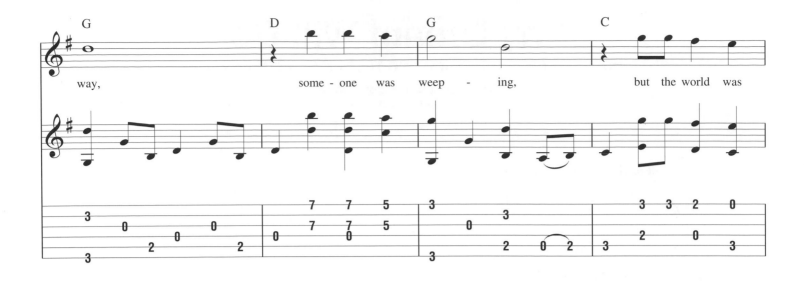

way, some - one was weep - ing, but the world was

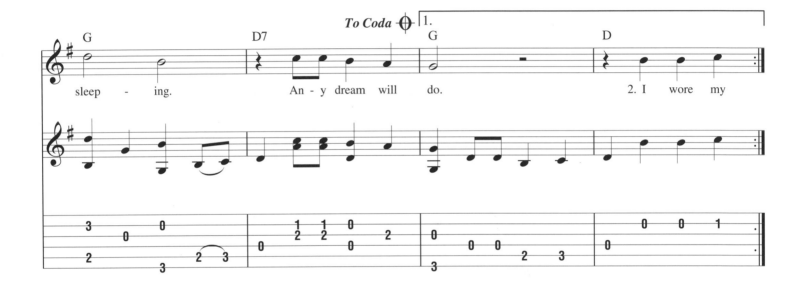

sleep - ing. An - y dream will do. 2. I wore my

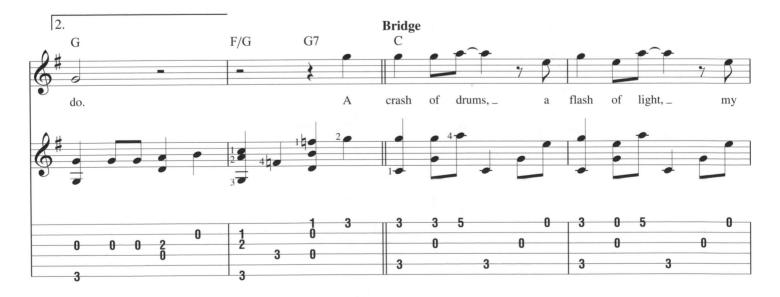

do. A crash of drums, _ a flash of light, _ my

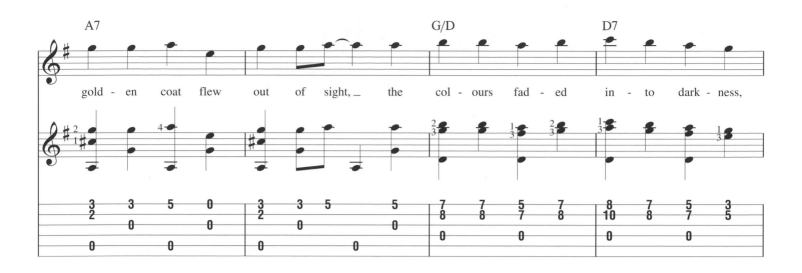

golden coat flew out of sight, __ the colours faded into darkness,

D.S. al Coda

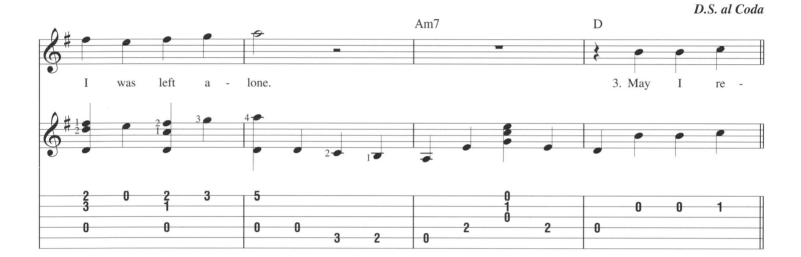

I was left a - lone.   3. May I re -

Coda

do,   an - y dream will do.

Additional Lyrics

2. I wore my coat with golden lining,
   Bright colours shining, wonderful and new.
   And in the east the dawn was breaking,
   The world was waking. Any dream will do.

3. May I return to the beginning,
   The light is dimming and the dream is too.
   The world and I, we are still waiting,
   Still hesitating. Any dream will do,
   Any dream will do.

Barney Theme Song

Traditional Music ("Yankee Doodle")
Lyrics by Stephen Bates Baltes and Philip A. Parker

Drop D tuning:
(low to high) D–A–D–G–B–E

Intro
Moderately

1. Bar - ney is a di - no - saur from
2., 3. *See additional lyrics*

our im - ag - i - na - tion and when he's tall he's what we call a

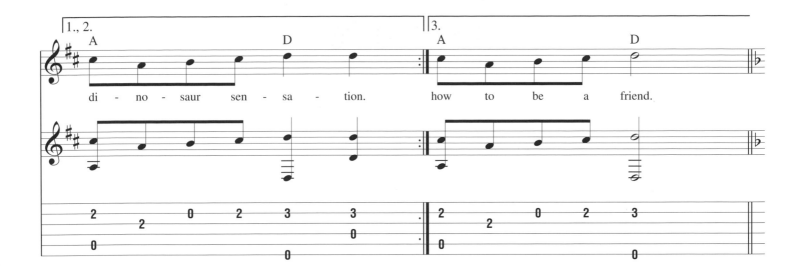

di - no - saur sen - sa - tion.   how to be a friend.

Chorus

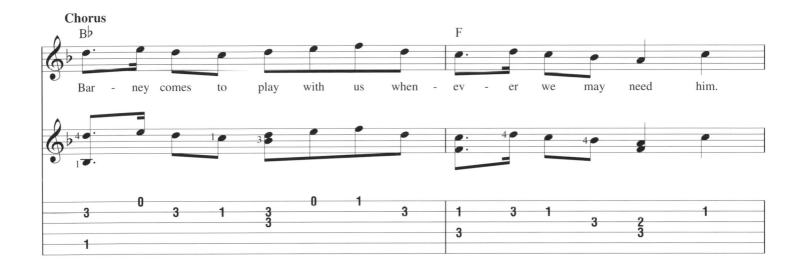

Bar - ney comes to play with us when - ev - er we may need him.

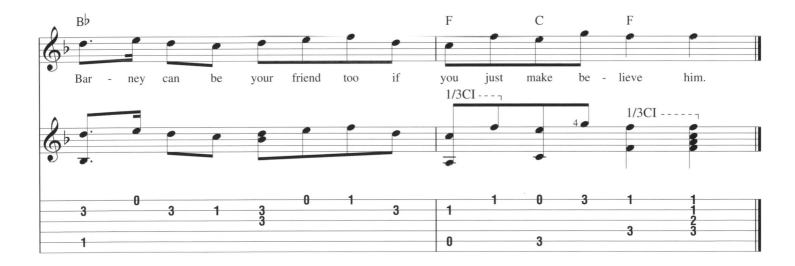

Bar - ney can be your friend too if you just make be - lieve him.

Additional Lyrics

2. Barney's friends are big and small; they come from lots of places:
   After school they meet to play and sing with happy faces.

3. Barney shows them lots of things like how to play pretend,
   A-B-C'S, and one-two-three's and how to be a friend.

Do-Re-Mi

from THE SOUND OF MUSIC

Lyrics by Oscar Hammerstein II
Music by Richard Rodgers

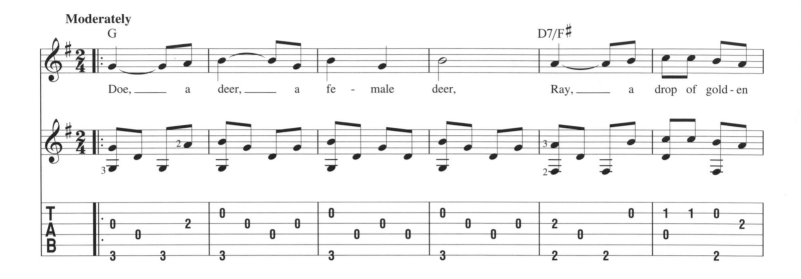

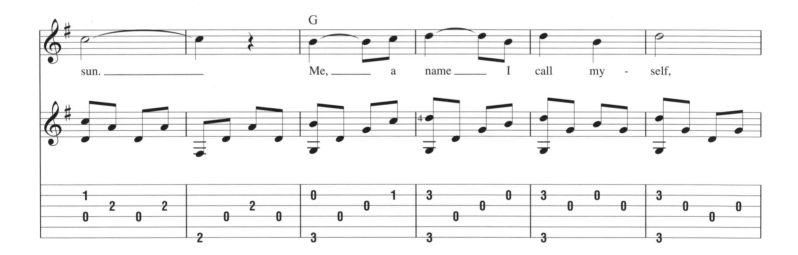

La,_____ a note to fol - low sew._____ Tea,_____ a

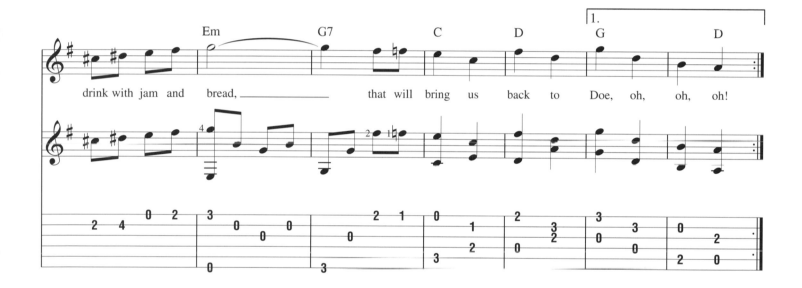

drink with jam and bread,_____ that will bring us back to Doe, oh, oh, oh!

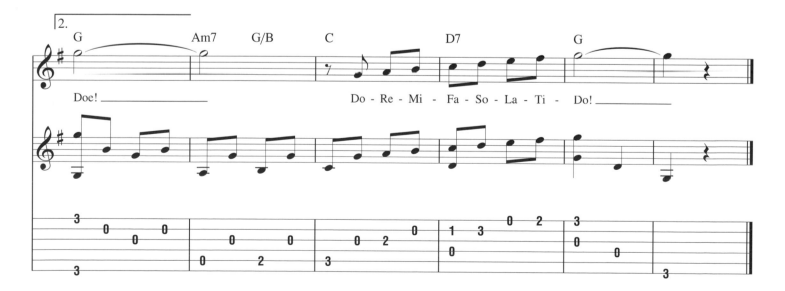

Doe!_____ Do - Re - Mi - Fa - So - La - Ti - Do!_____

It's a Small World

from "it's a small world" at Disneyland Park and Magic Kingdom Park

Words and Music by Richard M. Sherman and Robert B. Sherman

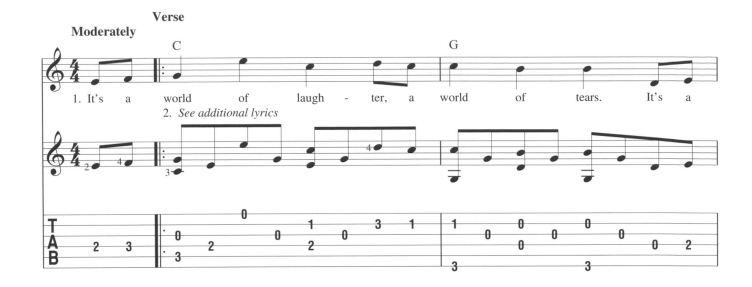

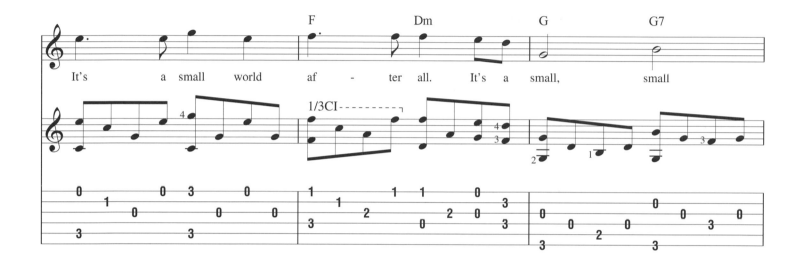

Additional Lyrics

2. There is just one moon and one golden sun,
   And a smile means friendship to ev'ryone.
   Though the mountains divide and the oceans are wide,
   It's a small world after all.

Linus and Lucy

By Vince Guaraldi

Drop D tuning:
(low to high) D–A–D–G–B–E

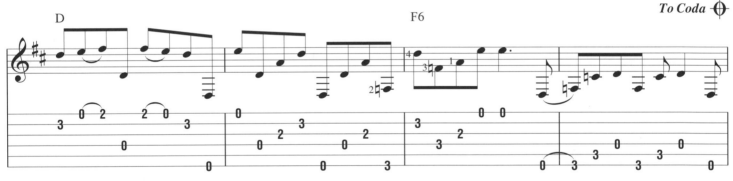

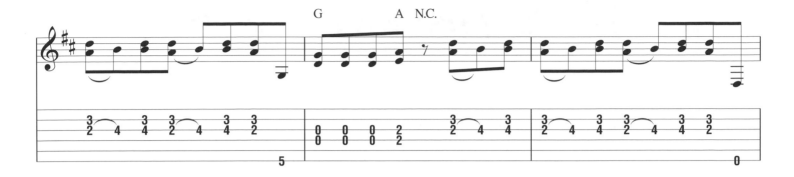

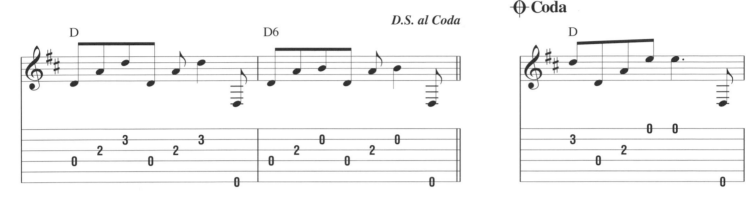

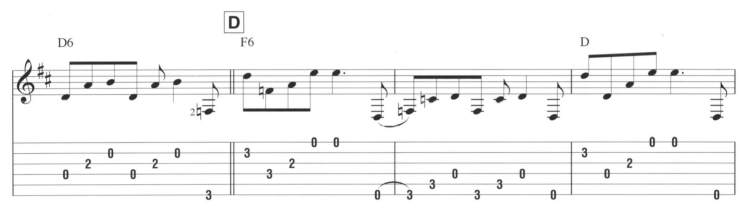

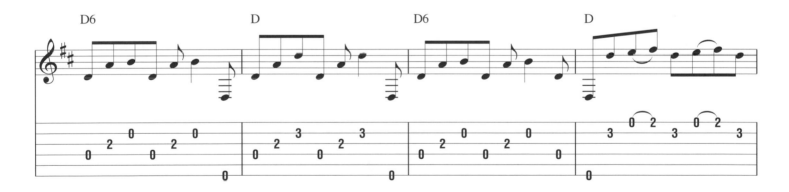

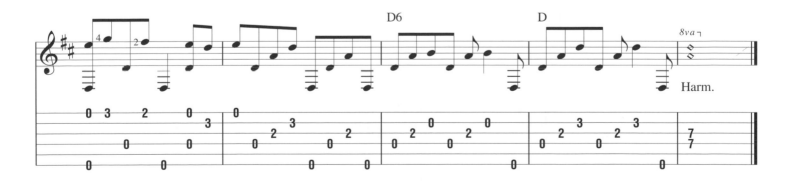

The Muppet Show Theme

from the Television Series

Words and Music by Jim Henson and Sam Pottle

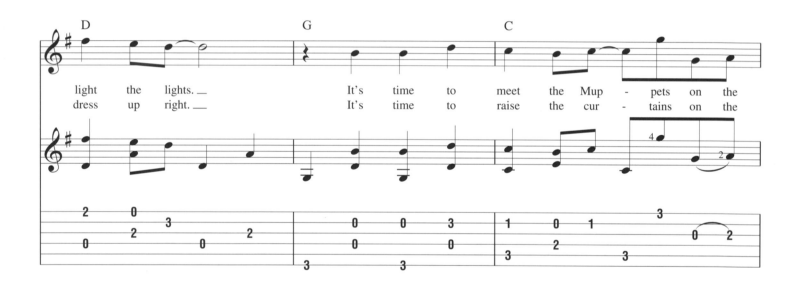

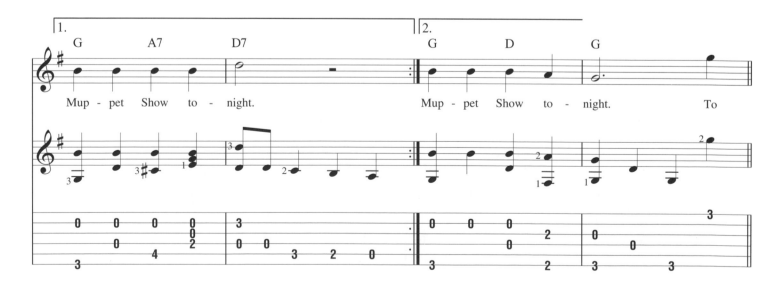

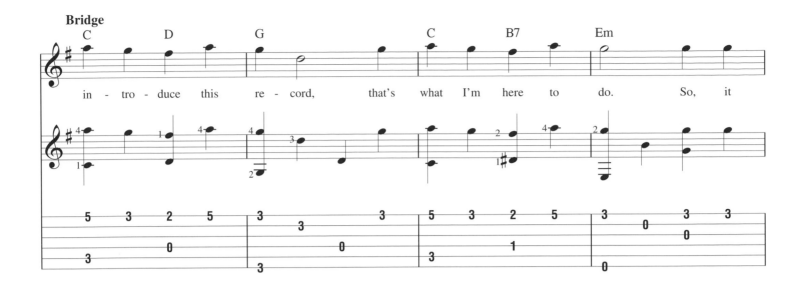

Bridge

in-tro-duce this re-cord, that's what I'm here to do. So, it

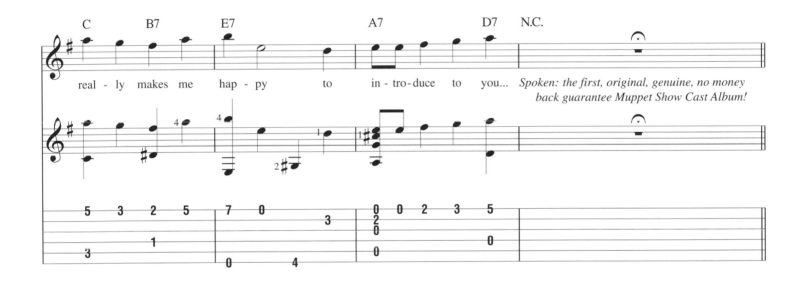

real-ly makes me hap-py to in-tro-duce to you... *Spoken: the first, original, genuine, no money back guarantee Muppet Show Cast Album!*

Verse

3. It's time to put on make-up. It's time to dress up right.＿

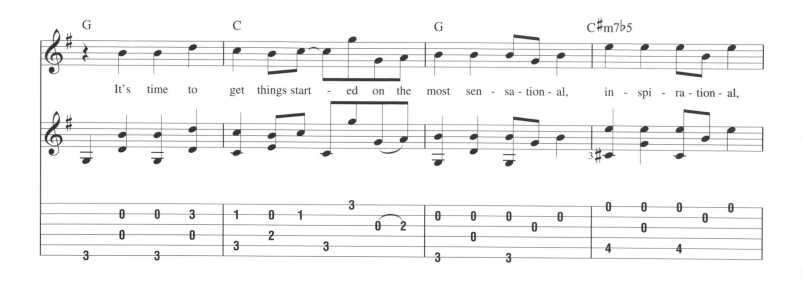

It's time to get things start - ed on the most sen - sa - tion - al, in - spi - ra - tion - al,

cel - e - bra - tion - al, mup - pet - a - tion - al. This is what we

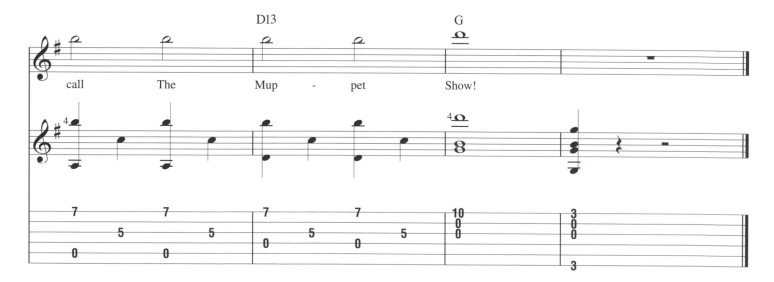

call The Mup - pet Show!

Puff the Magic Dragon

Words and Music by Lenny Lipton and Peter Yarrow

Verse
Moderately

1. Puff the mag - ic drag - on __ lived by __ the sea and
2., 3., 4. *See additional lyrics*

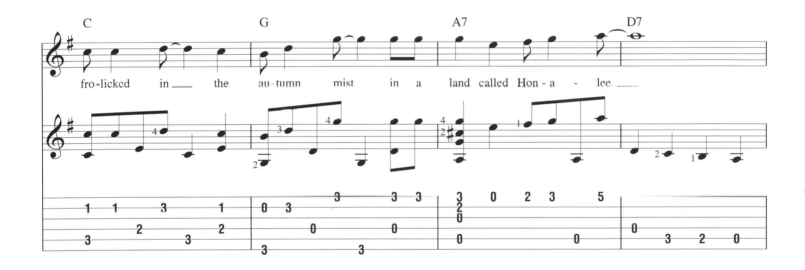

fro-licked in __ the au-tumn mist in a land called Hon - a - lee. __

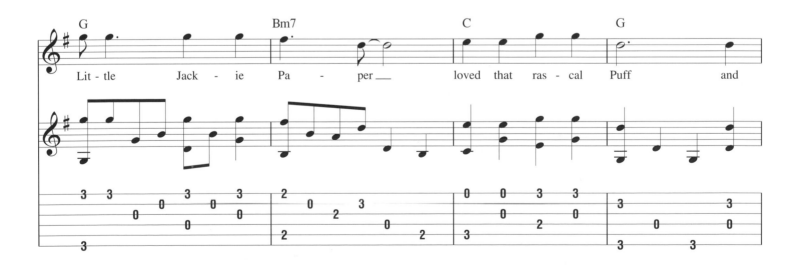

Lit - tle Jack - ie Pa - per __ loved that ras - cal Puff and

Chorus

18

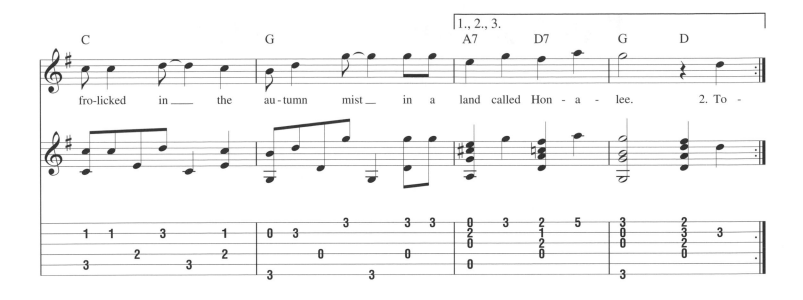

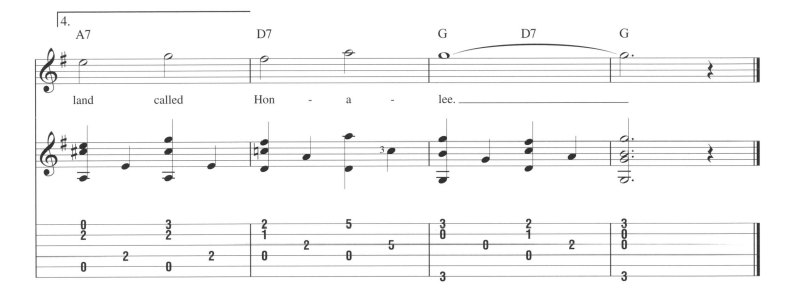

Additional Lyrics

2. Together they would travel on a boat with billowed sail.
   Jackie kept a lookout perched on Puff's gigantic tail.
   Noble kings and princes would bow when e'er they came.
   Pirate ships would low'r their flags when Puff roared out his name. Oh!

3. A dragon lives forever, but not so little boys.
   Painted wings and giant rings make way for other toys.
   One gray night it happened, Jackie Paper came no more,
   And Puff that mighty dragon, he ceased his fearless roar.

4. His head was bent in sorrow, green tears fell like rain.
   Puff no longer went to play along the Cherry Lane.
   Without his lifelong friend, Puff could not be brave,
   So Puff that mighty dragon sadly slipped into his cave. Oh!

The Return of Puff

Puff the magic dragon danced down the Cherry Lane.
He came upon a little girl, Julie Maple was her name.
She'd heard that Puff had gone away, but that can never be,
So together they went sailing to the land called Honalee.

The Rainbow Connection

from THE MUPPET MOVIE

Words and Music by Paul Williams and Kenneth L. Ascher

1. Why are there so man-y songs a-bout rain-bows, __ and what's on the
2., 3. *See additional lyrics*

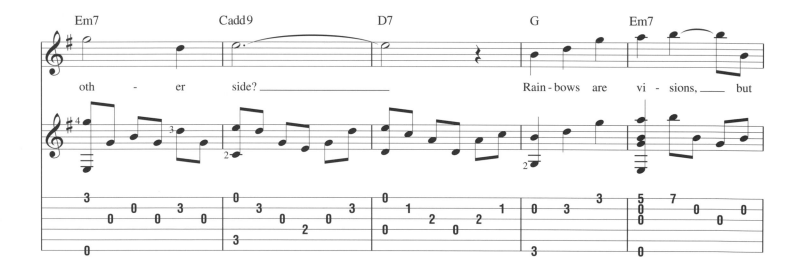

oth - er side? _____ Rain - bows are vi - sions, __ but

on - ly il - lu - sions, __ and rain - bows have noth - ing to hide. _____

Bridge

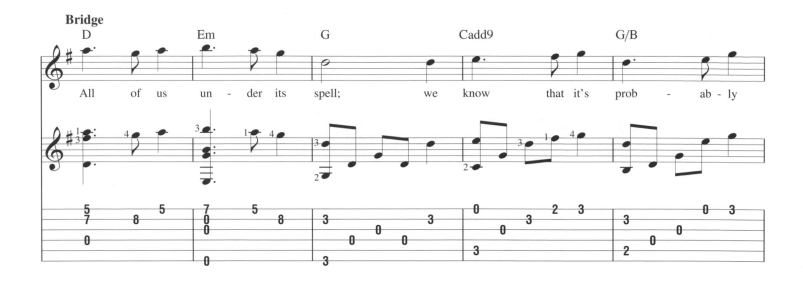

All of us un-der its spell; we know that it's prob-ab-ly

mag - ic.

D.C. al Coda

🜨 **Coda**

Outro

me. La, da, da,

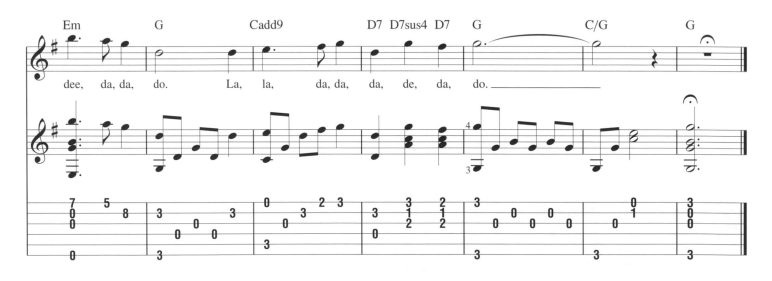

dee, da, da, do. La, la, da, da, da, de, da, do. _____

Additional Lyrics

2. Who said that ev'ry wish could be heard and answered
   When wished on the morning star?
   Somebody thought of that, and someone believed it;
   Look what it's done so far.
   What's so amazing that keeps us stargazing?
   And what do we think we might see?

3. Have you been half asleep and then you heard voices?
   I've heard them calling my name.
   Is this the sweet sound that calls the young sailors?
   The voice might be one and the same.
   I've heard it too many times to ignore it.
   It's someting that I'm s'posed to be.

Sesame Street Theme

Words by Bruce Hart, Jon Stone and Joe Raposo
Music by Joe Raposo

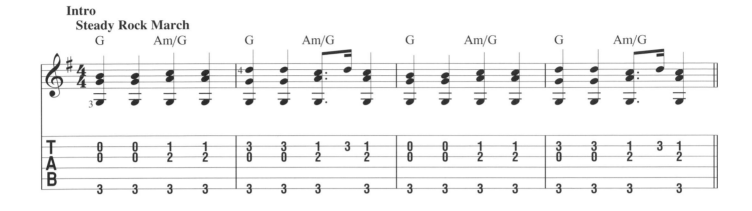

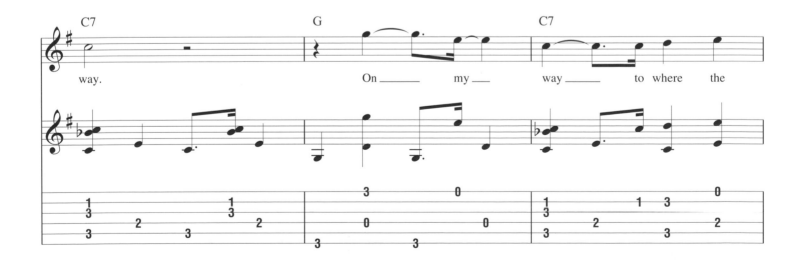

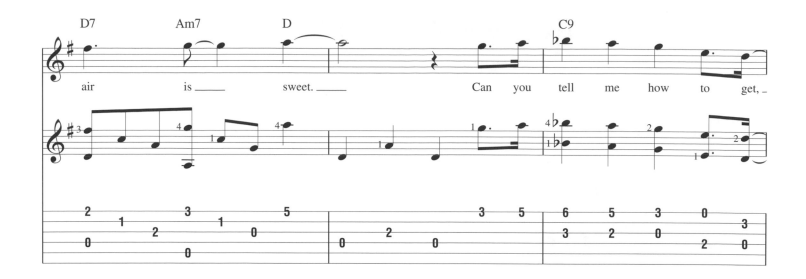

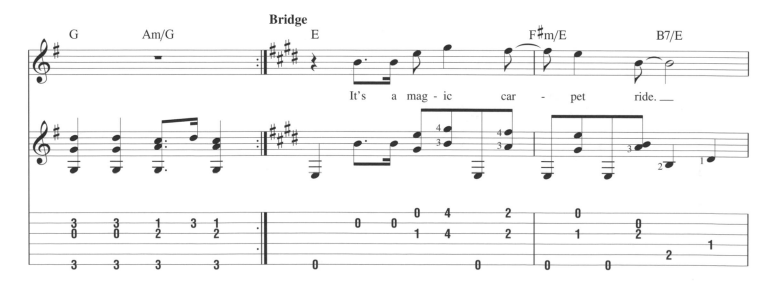

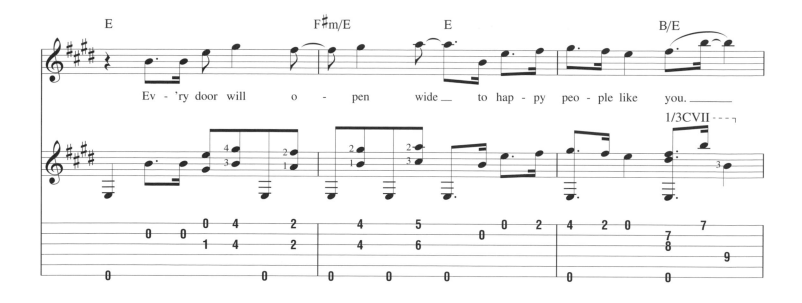

Ev - 'ry door will o - pen wide ___ to hap - py peo - ple like you. ___

D.S. al Coda

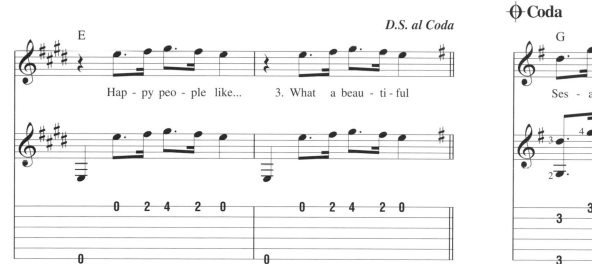

Hap - py peo - ple like...   3. What a beau - ti - ful

⊕ **Coda**

Ses - a - me Street? _

Outro

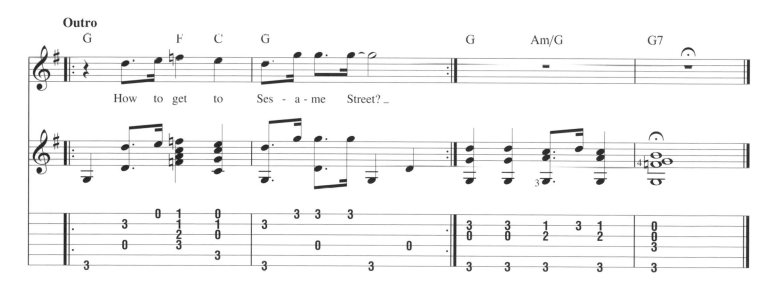

How to get to Ses - a - me Street? _

Additional Lyrics

2. Come and play! Everything's A-OK.
   Friendly neighbors there, that's where we meet.
   Can you tell me how to get,
   How to get to Sesame Street?

3. What a beautiful sunny day sweepin' the clouds away.
   On my way to where the air is sweet.
   Can you tell me how to get,
   How to get to Sesame Street?

Splish Splash

Words and Music by Bobby Darin and Murray Kaufman

Drop D tuning:
(low to high) D–A–D–G–B–E

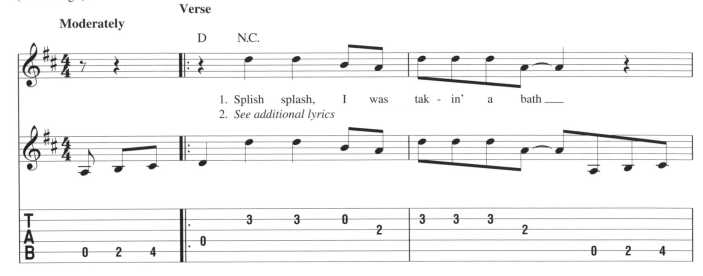

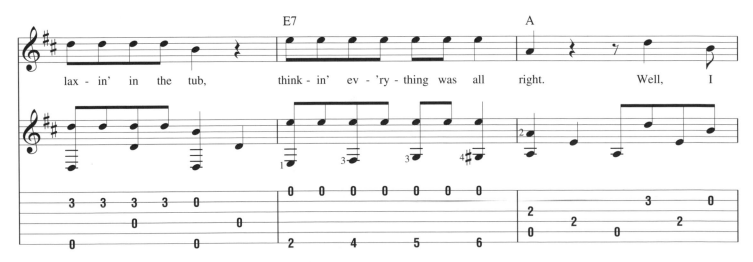

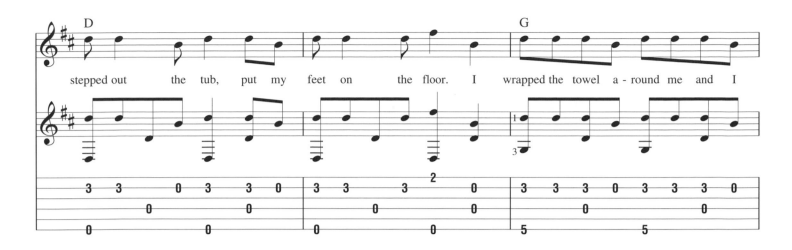

stepped out the tub, put my feet on the floor. I wrapped the towel a - round me and I

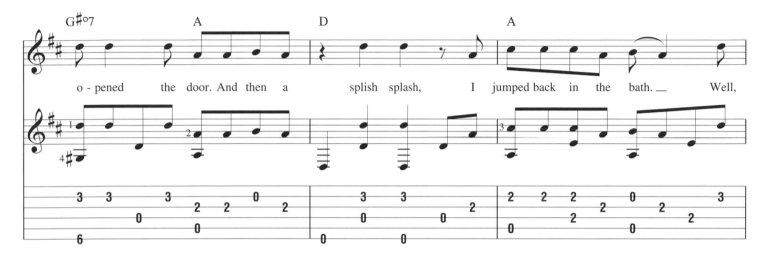

o - pened the door. And then a splish splash, I jumped back in the bath. __ Well,

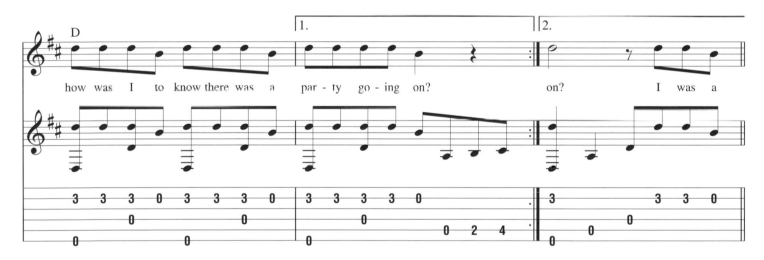

how was I to know there was a par - ty go - ing on? on? I was a

Outro

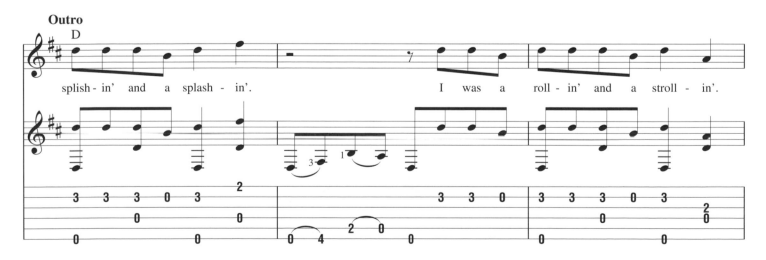

splish - in' and a splash - in'. I was a roll - in' and a stroll - in'.

Additional Lyrics

2. Bing bang, I saw the whole gang
   Dancin' on my livin' room rug. Yeah.
   Flip flop, they were doin' the bop;
   All the teens had the dancin' bug.
   There was Lollipop with Peggy Sue.
   Good golly, Miss Molly was a even there too.
   A well a, splish splash, I forgot about the bath.
   I went and put my dancing shoes on.

A Spoonful of Sugar

from Walt Disney's MARY POPPINS

Words and Music by Richard M. Sherman and Robert B. Sherman

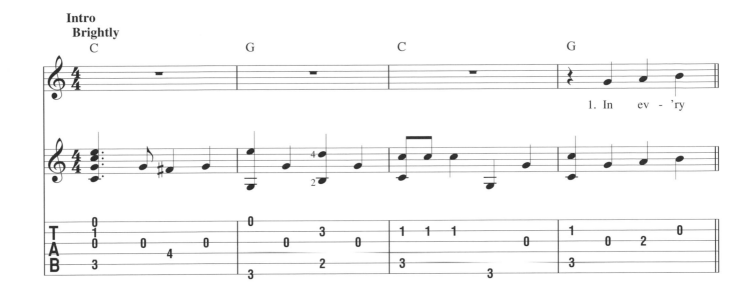

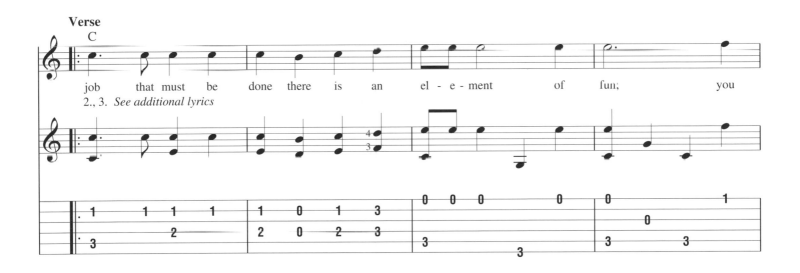

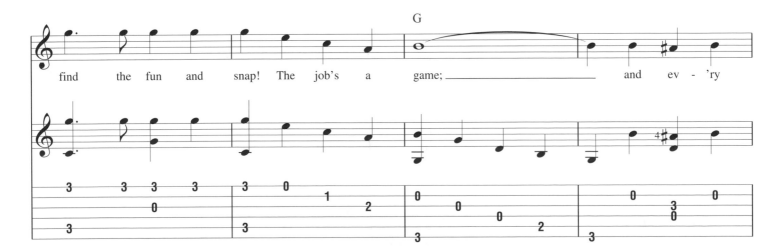

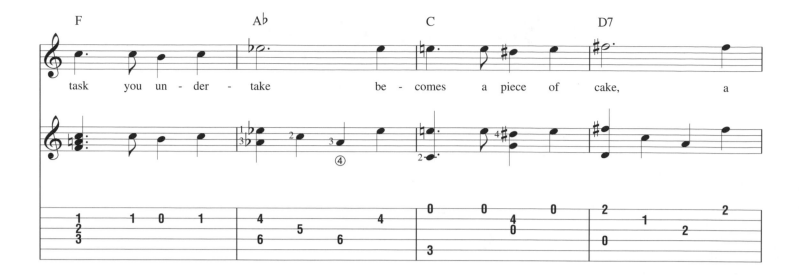

task   you   un - der - take   be - comes   a   piece   of   cake,   a

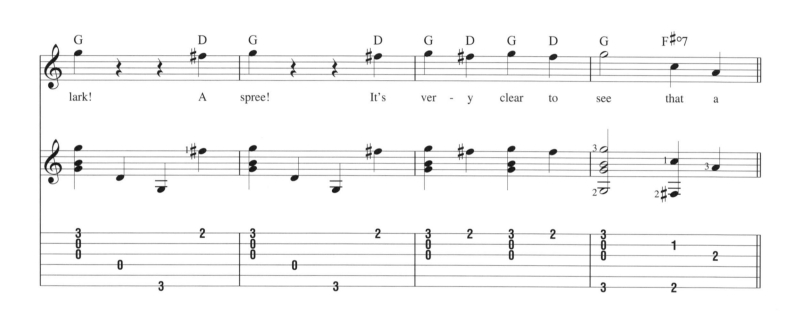

lark!   A   spree!   It's   ver - y   clear   to   see   that   a

Chorus

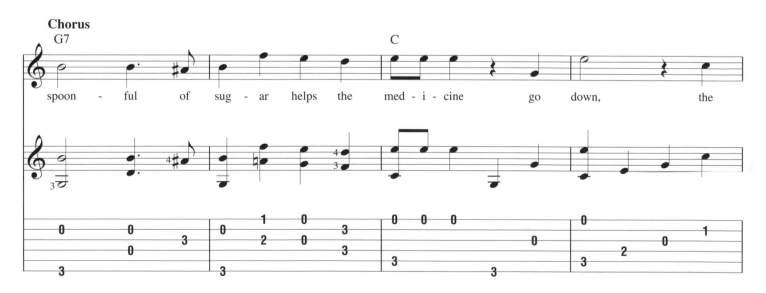

spoon - ful   of   sug - ar   helps   the   med - i - cine   go   down,   the

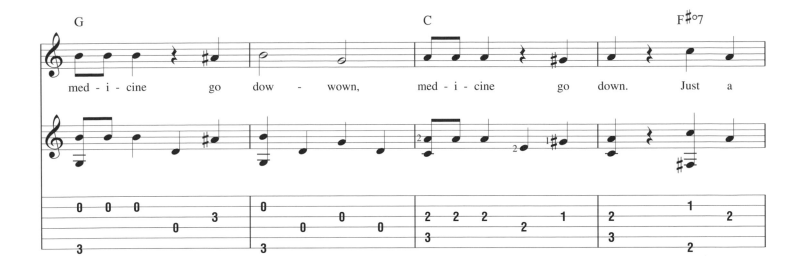

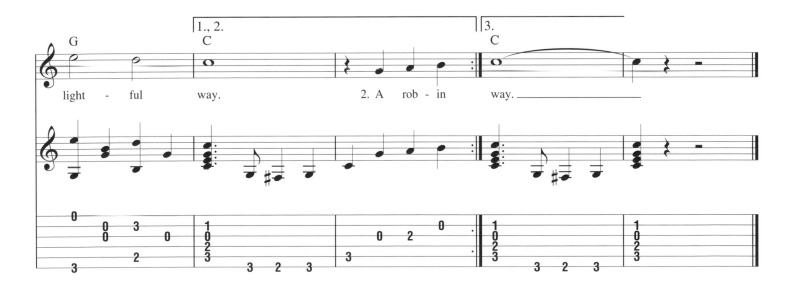

Additional Lyrics

2. A robin feathering his nest has very little time to rest
   While gathering his bits of twine and twig.
   Though quite intent in his pursuit, he has a merry tune to toot;
   He knows a song will move the job along.
   For a...

3. The honey bees that fetch the nectar from the flowers to the comb
   Never tire of ever buzzing to and fro,
   Because they take a little nip from ev'ry flower that they sip,
   And hence, they find their task is not a grind.
   For a...

Winnie the Pooh

from Walt Disney's THE MANY ADVENTURES OF WINNIE THE POOH

Words and Music by Richard M. Sherman and Robert B. Sherman

Drop D tuning:
(low to high) D–A–D–G–B–E

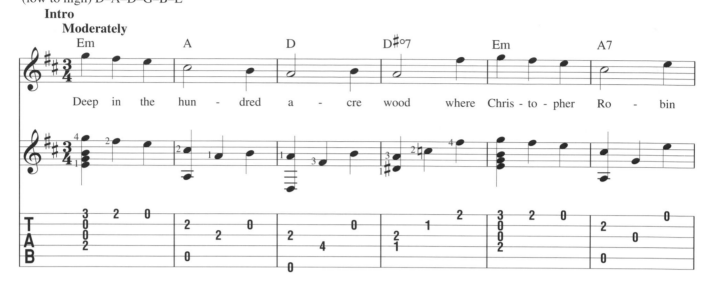

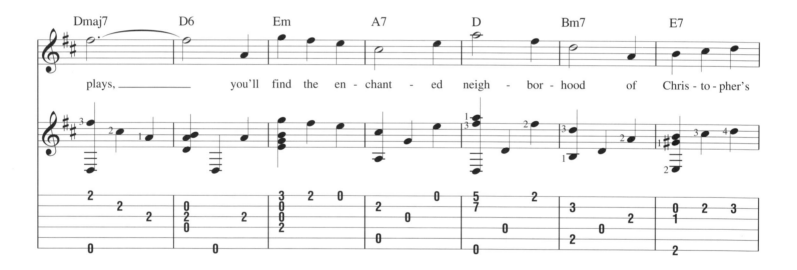

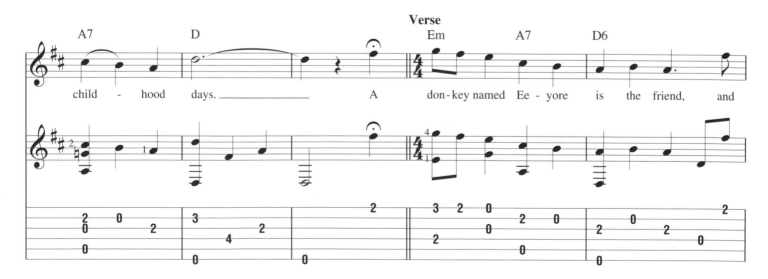

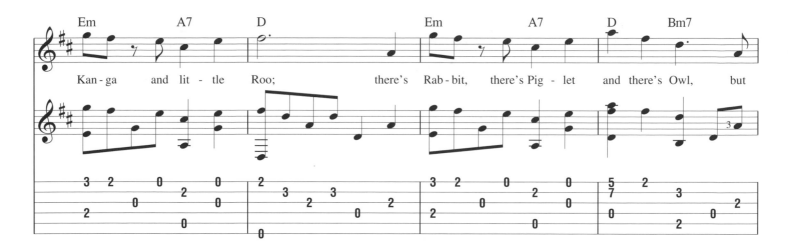

Kan - ga and lit - tle Roo; there's Rab - bit, there's Pig - let and there's Owl, but

Chorus

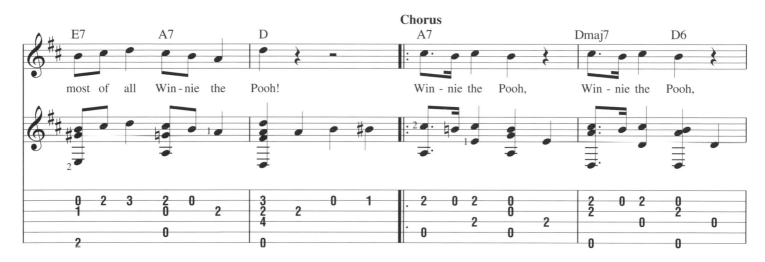

most of all Win - nie the Pooh! Win - nie the Pooh, Win - nie the Pooh,

tub - by lit tle cub - by all stuffed with fluff, he's Win - nie the Pooh,

Win - nie the Pooh, wil - ly, nil - ly, sil - ly ole bear. bear.

Won't You Be My Neighbor

(It's a Beautiful Day in This Neighborhood)

from MISTER ROGERS' NEIGHBORHOOD

Words and Music by Fred Rogers

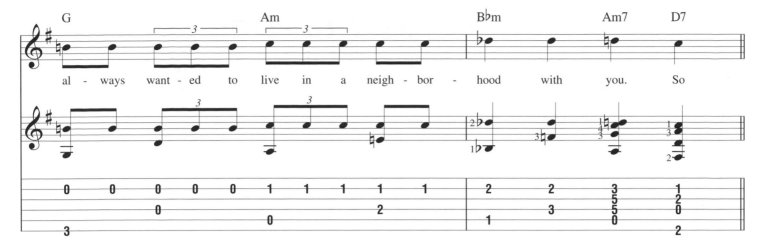

al - ways want - ed to live in a neigh - bor - hood with you. So

Outro-Verse

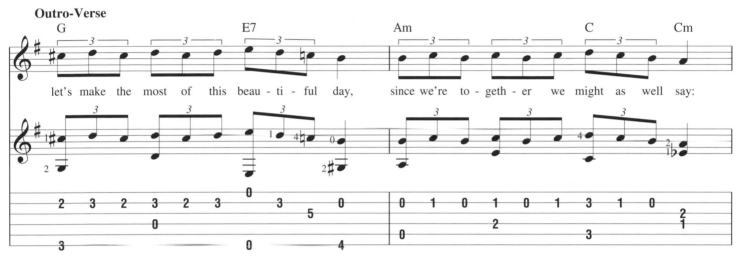

let's make the most of this beau - ti - ful day, since we're to - geth - er we might as well say:

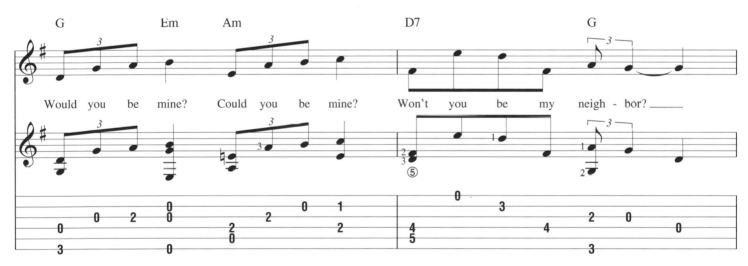

Would you be mine? Could you be mine? Won't you be my neigh - bor? _____

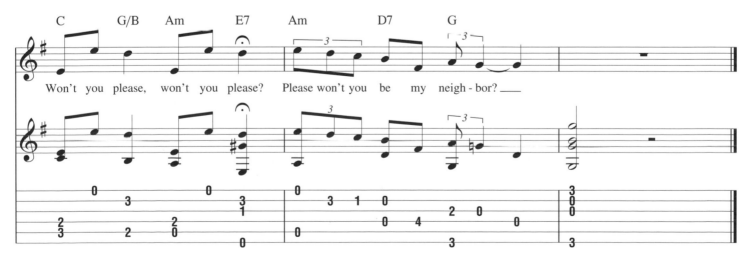

Won't you please, won't you please? Please won't you be my neigh - bor? ___

Zip-A-Dee-Doo-Dah

from Walt Disney's SONG OF THE SOUTH
from Disneyland and Walt Disney World's SPLASH MOUNTAIN

Words by Ray Gilbert
Music by Allie Wrubel

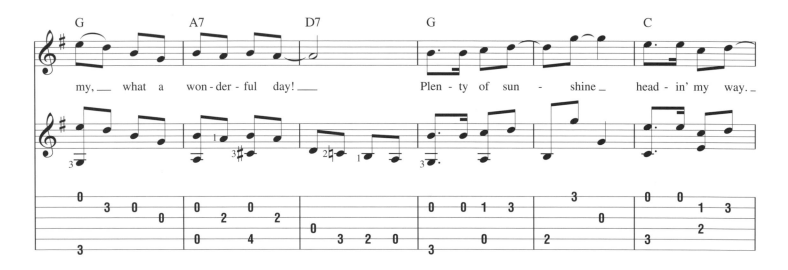

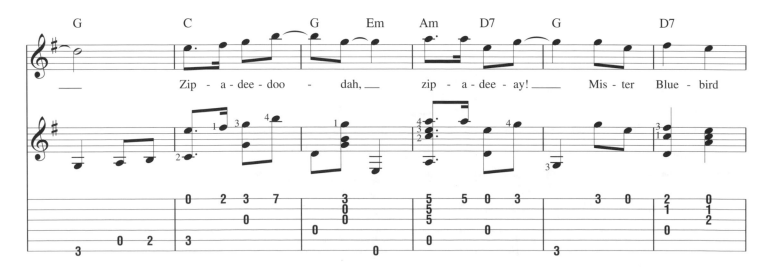

on my should - er, _____ it's the truth, _____ it's "act - ch'll" _ ev -'ry-thing is

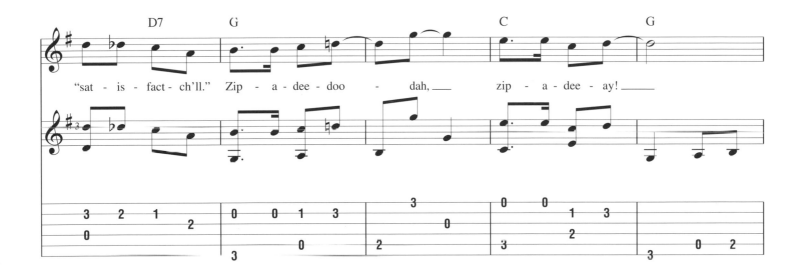

"sat - is - fact - ch'll." Zip - a - dee - doo - dah, _____ zip - a - dee - ay! _____

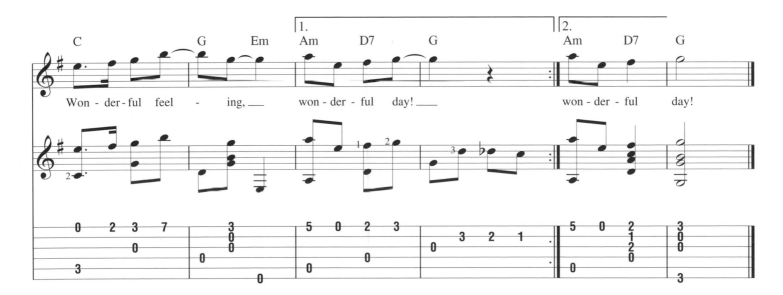

Won - der - ful feel - ing, _____ won - der - ful day! _____ won - der - ful day!

Yellow Submarine

Words and Music by John Lennon and Paul McCartney

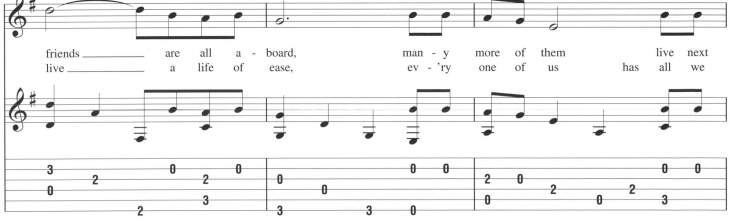